I R
Perfumed
Garden

THE
IRISH
Perfumed
Garden

Seamus All

Futura

A Futura Book

Copyright © Victorama 1987

First published in Great Britain in 1986
by Futura Publications

ISBN 0 7088 3270 9

Typeset by Leaper & Gard Ltd, Bristol, England
Printed in Great Britain by
Hazell, Watson & Viney Ltd, Aylesbury, Bucks.

Futura Publications
A Division of
Macdonald & Co (Publishers) Ltd
Greater London House
Hampstead Road
London NW1 7QX
A BPCC plc Company

Dedication

This book is dedicated to Mary Whitehouse
without whom everything is possible.

CONTENTS

(not in numerical order)

CONTENTS

(in numerical order)

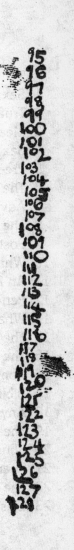

THE
ALTERNATIVE
CONTENTS

A
FOREWORD

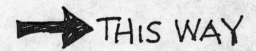 THIS WAY

SEX FOR
THE BEGINNER

SEX FOR THE SELF-STARTER

Simple questions for starters

What is sex?
Sex is an act performed by at least two people and lasting between thirty seconds and ten hours.

What is unnatural sex?
Unnatural sex is an act performed by at least two people and lasting under thirty seconds or over twelve days.

Who does it?
Either (a) a man and a woman
      (b) a man and a man
      (c) a woman and a woman
      (d) an official of the High Church of Scotland and a farmyard animal.

Where do they do it?
(See *News of the World* for full details.)

How do they do it?
(See *News of the World* for full details.)

What is the greatest number of people who can have sex at the same time?
(See Vicki Hodge for full details.)

What are the dangers of having sex?
Any of the following: pregnancy, AIDS, herpes, guilt complex, divorce, blackmail, death.

What are the dangers of not having sex?
(See Cliff Richard for full details.)

Irish Contraceptive Advice

For those living in the Irish Republic where conventional contraceptive devices are unavailable simply use the following technique to avoid unwanted pregnancy:

1. Before retiring to the bedchamber place a large wheelbarrow full of fresh cattle dung at the bottom of the bed.

2.   Now try making love with that there.

Where risk of pregnancy persists increase the number of wheelbarrows until all carnal instincts are extinguished.

The sex maniac's crossword

Well come on, when did a sex maniac ever mess around doing crosswords?

The world's dirtiest joke*

Russell 1: Russell.

Russell 2: Yes, pet?

Russell 1: Russell, can I ask you a question?

Russell 1: Only, it's a bit personal ...

Russell 2: No, no, go ahead pet, I don't mind.

Russell 1: Well, how long ... how long can you hold an erection for?

Russell 2: Well pet ... it all depends whose it is; doesn't it!

* In fact this is only the world's third most dirty joke, the other two being unsuitable for print owing to the country's strict censorship laws and also owing to the libel law relating to cases concerning Viscount Whitelaw.

Do it yourself dirty cartoons

Opposite you will find all you need to prepare your very own dirty cartoons: a box in which to place your drawing (the box is essential to avoid your drawing going on too far and filling up the whole page!) plus a line on which to write your funny caption. All you need to do is supply the drawings and joke and hey presto you have your very own personal cartoon. Plus you can make it just as dirty as you like and never mind any snooty-nosed publishers telling you you can't possibly put anything as rude as that in!!!

insert your line here

_____

insert your line here

_____

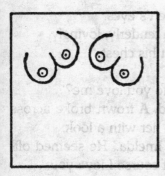

insert your line here

_____

insert your line here

_____

2
TRUE ROMANCES

Dip into the perfumed world of romantic fiction with this specially written short story by Barbara Carthouse.

True Romance

MILLS & BOON & MURPHY

Imelda gazed into Rupert's eyes.

'Rupert ...?' She spoke tenderly, lovingly.

Rupert held her against his chest.

'Yes, Imelda ...?'

'Rupert ... do you ... do you love me?'

Rupert seemed worried. A frown broke across his mouth and he caught her with a look.

'What a silly question, Imelda.' He seemed off-hand, almost irritated. 'Of course I love you. ...'

Imelda paused for a second, reassured.

'Rupert ...?'

Rupert looked into her eyes again.

'Yes?'

'Rupert, how much do you love me?'

Rupert raised an eyebrow and frowned.

'Why, with all my heart,' he gasped.

Imelda frowned.

'And how much is that?'

Rupert pulled away.

'What?'

Imelda caught her breath again.

'How much is it?' She seemed insistent, determined. 'Exactly how much is that?'

Rupert seemed baffled.

'Well, it's more than words can say.'

Imelda still seemed worried.

'Yes, Rupert,' she sighed, 'but quantitatively, how much is it? Is it this much? Or this much … or this much …?'

She moved her hands like a fisherman indicating the possibilities on offer.

'Well, I just love you, you can't measure how much … you can't say I love someone so much, and put a figure on it. If you love someone you love them, that's all there is to it. …' Rupert spoke as though he wished the conversation were finished.

Imelda seemed troubled. Her face was lined with thought.

'But people's love for each other grows?'

Rupert nodded.

'Yes.'

'Therefore you must be able to measure it. You must be able to put it on a chart and see how much it's growing!'

Rupert gave a deep sigh and clicked his teeth.

'All right, I love you very very very very very very very much!' There was a finality in his voice that seemed to pull down a veil on the whole matter.

He looked up. Imelda was clearly uncertain, her face was lost in thought and she ran her fingers along the table rail several times.

'It's still not very accurate, is it Rupert?'

Her voice carried with it a note of petulance.

Rupert could feel himself losing control and fought hard to check himself lest he spoke ill.

'It's just not very easy to quantify, that's all.' He found he was speaking with a voice of reason. 'You can't measure it in feet or inches. There isn't a universal measure of affection. You can't say I'll have two pounds of your best English love ...!'

Imelda drew back defensively as Rupert's tone rose.

'I only wanted to know approximately.'

Rupert paused, calculated his thoughts, and spoke.

'All right. I love you thirty-six inches.'

Imelda's jaw dropped at once.

'What?'

'I love you thirty-six inches.'

Imelda tried hard to concentrate for she thought maybe it was she that was at fault.

'Well, what does that mean?!'

Her voice carried with it a pained expression.

Rupert took note of this and continued,

'You were the one who wanted me to measure my love, so there you are ... that's how much I love you ... thirty-six inches!'

A trace of hope ran across Imelda's face.

'What's that in millimetres?'

Rupert sank back in a morass of anxiety.

'I don't know ...' He scowled, sat, stood, then took a pencil in his hand ...

'Thirty-six inches make a yard, and a yard is nearly a metre, and a metre is 1000 millimetres ... therefore I love you ... nearly 1000 millimetres ...!'

Imelda looked on disapprovingly.

'It still doesn't seem very much.'

Rupert felt frustration well up inside him.

'Well, of course it doesn't ... that's why I said you can't measure it ... because if you do measure it then it doesn't seem very much!!!'

Imelda held a handkerchief to her eyes.

'So you're blaming me?'

Rupert looked on aghast.

'What?'

'You're blaming me, is that it?'

Imelda pressed home her advantage on the hapless Rupert. Rubert groaned.

'No, of course I'm not saying that!'

Imelda wasn't to be outshone.

'You're saying it was all my fault, aren't you?'
Rupert fought back, his tongue unleashed.

'I'm not saying that at all!'

'You're implying it though.' Imelda wasn't to be outdone.

'No, I'm not.' Rupert wore a look of horror.

'Yes, you are. Look, what are you trying to say?'

Rupert took Imelda's hand and held it in his own.

'I'm not trying to say anything, Imelda.'

Imelda pulled her hand away.

'Yes, you are, you're trying to say that you don't love me, aren't you!'

'Of course I'm not.'

Rupert fought to defend his innocence. He bit his lip and turned squarely on Imelda who now lay sobbing on the floor.

'Look, I love you Imelda, I really and truly love you ... I love you more than words can ever say ...'

Imelda paused, and wiped the tears away from her red-rimmed eyes. At last she stopped sobbing and put the handkerchief away.

'You do love me?'

Rupert smiled, confident again.

'Of course I love you darling.'

Imelda's face seemed happier now, her eyes no longer bore the traces of uncertainty and she drew Rupert towards her.

'Rupert!'

Rupert smiled into her eyes.

'Yes, Imelda?'

'Rupert ... how much do you actually love me?'

THE END

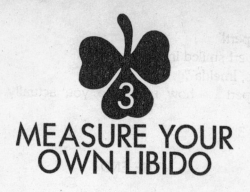

MEASURE YOUR OWN LIBIDO

Measure your own libido

Don't be caught out! Measure your sexual drive before you start. A simple question-and-answer section allows you to measure your own libido from the comfort of your own bidet. Start at the top of the column opposite and colour up as far as the recorded score. Note down the results and diagnose your own sex profile. Tear out and send to prospective bed partners to ensure complete compatibility. Avoids unnecessary disappointment.

In my life I have had x partners

0 1 2 50 100 200 1000 2000 45,000,000

Preferred number of people in bed together (including yourself)

0   1   2   3   4   5   10   20   200

Breast measurements (woman)

28 30 32 34 36 38 40 44 78

Breast measurements (man)

28 30 32 34 36 38 40 44 78

Waist measurements

78 44 40 38 32 30 28 26 24

Normal duration of love making

| 30 secs | 1 min | 1 min 27 secs | 3 min | 5 min | ½ hr | 2 hrs | 5 hrs | 5 days |

	30 secs		78		28		28		0		0
	1 min		44		30		30		1		1
	1 min 27 secs		40		32		32		2		2
	3 min		38		34		34		3		50
	5 min		32		36		36		4		100
	½ hr		30		38		38		5		200
	2 hrs		28		40		40		10		1000
	5 hrs		26		44		44		20		2000
	5 days		24		78		78		200		45,000,000

Well-developed sex profile

Less well-developed sex profile

(BRITISH)

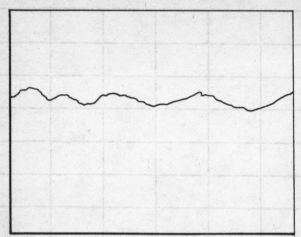

Time ▷

Most people have a sexual cycle like this

Time ▷

This is the cycle for someone with high sexual drive

26

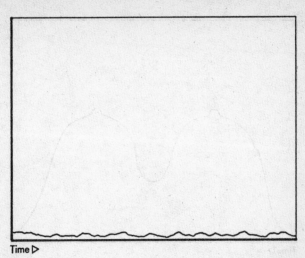

Time ▷

This is the cycle for someone with low sexual drive

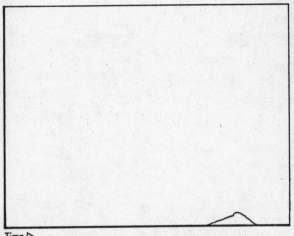

Time ▷

This is the cycle for a typical quantity surveyor

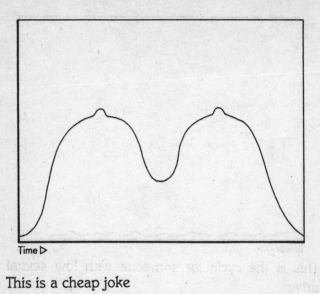

Time ▷

This is a cheap joke

4
SEX AND
THE HUMAN BODY

A doctor writes:

mr. mr — r!

Now somebody else writes because no one can read a word the doctor writes:

'For the purposes of sex the human body can be divided into two halves — the erogenous half, and the non-erogenous half. Or rather the erogenous 1% and the non-erogenous 99%. The trick lies in finding the erogenous 1%. Start with a few elementary guidelines — erogenous zones are unlikely to be found in the area shown overleaf.'

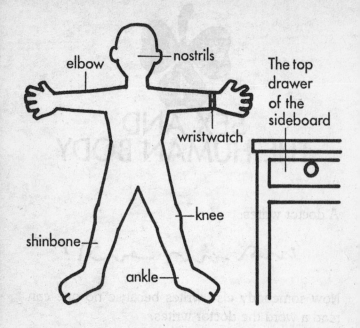

elbow

nostrils

wristwatch

The top
drawer
of the
sideboard

knee

shinbone

ankle

Here is a simple table. Fill it in and keep it.
Hand it to any new partner upon introduction.

Part of the body (include diagram):_____

Name and position: _____

State level of arousal when touched: _____
(e.g. 'more aroused than a cold teabag'
'marginally less arousing than a walk through
seaweed' ...)

Remember sexual activity is a physical act and should be prepared for accordingly. The human body needs to prepare and train for love-making as it would do for any other sport:

- Never make love on a full stomach (especially someone else's.)

- As you get older you will find your body takes longer to respond. Accommodate this by beginning any act of love-making several days before you wish to climax.

- Do not make love when you have high blood pressure. To avoid high blood pressure check exactly when the lady's husband will be coming home before you begin.

- Making love burns up the same number of calories as riding a bicycle for five miles. Think how far you could ride your bike before beginning and match your love life to this target.

  (Note: These figures are based on an average bike journey. There is no bicycle ride that goes for fifty miles downhill continuously and your calculations should not be based on figures thus calculated.)

  (This explains the expression *on your bike* meaning literally to go off and engage in sexual activity ... i.e. **** off!)

31

Male and female bodies

Learn how to distinguish the two apart. Note that in the case of Eastern European female athletes there is no difference. Try and discover which type of body you possess. Write the answer down on a piece of paper and keep it by your side constantly should you need it for reference. Try and identify the major differences between the two types of body. Keep trying. You'll be surprised how much fun it can be.

Sexy Battleships: A new game!

The winner is the one who manages to sink his battleship first!!

Instructions: Both competitors should draw up a chart like the one above. They then take it in turns to call out a square at a time using the grid reference, having first marked their most sensual area with a cross. Thus in the case above if the big toe on the left foot was the zone of greatest arousal, a cross would be put in square 201. Should a player identify his fellow player's 'sexy zone' they should both take their

clothes off and investigate further. If the square is not identified after 30 seconds they should still both take their clothes off!

The human body

Vital facts ...

The ten least common ruptures are of

1. The nose
2. The head
3. The earlobe
4. The forehead
5. The left nipple
6. The right nipple
7. The greased nipple
8. The camping stove
9. The electric toothbrush
10. The pyjama bottom's cord

The world's least common ailments are

1. Housemaid's ear
2. Ruptured tongue
3. Nasal colic
4. Navel colic
5. Royal Naval colic
6. Royal Naval bum
7. Scoutmaster's bum
8. Terminal toothache
9. Ingrowing brain
10. Politician's brain

The ten least common ways of performing a lobotomy are

1. By hypnosis
2. By post
3. By luck
4. With a crowbar
5. With ten pints of Watneys inside you
6. With a stick of gelignite
7. With a pair of traction engines
8. In a public phone box
9. On roller skates
10. On the National Health

The ten organs least often required for transplant surgery are

1. The chin
2. The scrotum
3. The foot
4. The nostrils
5. The breasts (male)
6. The underarm hair
7. The elbow
8. The rectum
9. The toenails
10. The head

The ten most unusual places to find warts are

1. On the bathmat
2. On the sideboard
3. Underneath the sideboard
4. Inside a family-size tin of beans
5. In a delicatessen's in Chepstow
6. On the inside of a willy-warmer
7. On the underneath of a butter dish
8. Next door to Sainsbury's
9. On Wayne Sleep's bum
10. Bulgaria

The ten least common causes of a headache are

1. Fish in the atmosphere
2. Standing near wet cardboard
3. Wearing rubber insoles
4. Living in a house with French windows
5. Having Nigerian neighbours
6. Driving a car with tubeless tyres
7. Proximity to a large piece of pork pie
8. Too-tight combinations
9. 12" nail through the head
10. Sexual relations with a geologist

The ten worst alternatives to wearing a crepe bandage are wearing a bandage made of

1. Old muddy rugby socks
2. Back copies of the *Radio Times*
3. The wrappers from three Bounty bars
4. Old plastic trays from Chinese takeaways
5. Damp carpet tiles
6. Secondhand toilet paper
7. Rotted seaweed
8. Bus tickets
9. Old copies of the *Sun* crossword puzzle
10. The labels off the back of five Rice Krispie packets

The ten least common ways of performing a partial hysterectomy are by

1. Magnetism
2. Monthly instalments
3. With a radish
4. On a snooker table
5. In the penalty box at Old Trafford
6. Without hands
7. With a Moulinex food mixer
8. During the heats of *It's A Knock-Out*
9. By a homosexual one-eyed illiterate vicar from Hull
10. On stilts

5
PRE-CARNAL PRACTICES

Many people forget that the act of congress (not to be confused with an Act of Congress which is the name given to any addition made to the US statute book) involves considerable preparatory enjoyment, often called foreplay or the pre-strump.

Traditional pre-carnal practices include dinner at an expensive restaurant/soft lights/romantic music/a car which suddenly runs out of petrol. However more recently foreplay has followed the paths of such fads as Nouvelle Cuisine, New Celibacy and New Romanticism and there now comes the generation of new carnalists who are dedicated to new or radically different forms of foreplay, including:

- dinner at a very cheap restaurant or Wimpy,

- harsh lights including two 150 watt light bulbs with no shades,

- German oompah music played very loudly, and

- a London Transport double-decker bus that suddenly runs out of petrol.

For the more traditional carnalist the following however applies. Having lured your escort to the bedchamber the procedure is:

1. Remove your clothes (vital for full enjoyment).
2. Remove your partner's clothes (also vital for full enjoyment).
3. Avoid carefully hanging up all your clothes in the wardrobe taking a full ten minutes to sort out your sock drawer on the way.
4. Leap into bed having first taken care to remove the hot-water bottle and the piece of buttered toast in there since last Thursday.
5. Switch off the light and put on the oompah music.

The County Clare lonely hearts column

71-YEAR-OLD VIRGIN, waiting for the right man to come along, now seeks anything in a pair of trousers that moves.

WOMAN with eye for men would like to meet man with eye for women with a view to putting both eyes together and making a pair.

STEAMY hot 98-year-old redhead (no hair, just red head) would like to meet an old man with a view to a not very long-term relationship.

DISCERNING man wishes to meet elegant sophisticated woman for opera, ballet, intellectual discussion, and a good old bonk.

MAN who thinks he's a piece of cottage cheese on the end of a knife wishes to meet a woman who thinks she's crackers.

FOOTBALL fan, two legs, long balls, dribbler, seeks to make a pass at female supporter, no draws, two points, holds everything in the air, with a view to scoring.

TOUGH hard hairy green gooseberry wishes to be whisked away to make a fool of itself.

TALL virile man ... sensual, seeks one night of unforgettable passion. Wishes to meet 364 other women for full training session.

BENDO— the incredible India-rubber man — wishes to meet female contortionist with a view to seeing each other's point of view.

REALIST — 4'8", buck teeth, big nose, acne, National Health glasses — wishes to meet bloke who will drop her after just five minutes.

EIGHT-LEGGED man with face like a kipper seeks date with four very short-sighted girls or a very understanding octopus ... photo definitely not required.

ME? I'm tough, rough, rugged, clean. I look good. I feel good, my body is covered in muscles and packed with power. I have an absolutely amazing appetite for love and I know you'll agree I'm just about the meanest sex machine there has ever been. You? You're the sort of chick who can put up with bullshit like this!!!

WOMAN with three eyes wishes to meet gent with same with a view to seeing eye-to-eye-to-eye.

MAN — James Dean eyes, James Dean hair, James Dean nose, James Dean figure, speaks like James Dean, dresses like James Dean — wishes to meet woman to accompany him on very short motoring holiday.

IRANIAN gentleman, devout follower of the Koran, wishes to meet woman with a view to a spot of how's-your-father's-brother's-mother's-cousin's-first friend's uncle's-ass.

HI! Are you looking for a guy who's aged between 25 and 30, has a sensational physique, tanned skin, blonde hair, blue eyes, and a fabulous hairy chest? You are? Well that's funny ... so am I!

WOMAN with complete chronological table of the kings and queens of England tattooed on her body wishes to meet gentleman with particular interest in the House of Stuart and the House of Orange.

JEWISH gentleman, no drawbacks, wishes to meet woman who will understand his predicament.

NYMPHOMANIAC, working her way through all males in the London telephone director, urgently needs to get in touch with Mr Zebeedee Zyzniewski.

SPINSTER, 83, waiting for 'Mr Right' to come along — now willing to consider offers from Mr Completely-And-Utterly-Wrong as well.

MAN with 100 testicles wishes to meet very understanding woman. Alternatively wishes to find employment as a fully self-contained bingo hall caller.

STUD for hire. Hi, I'm Britain's leading stud and I'm available for hire every night of the week. Except Wednesday, because that's when I go to my asthma clinic.

BIG chesty tart who bonks like the clappers wishes to meet red-hot geezer for a quick knob or two ... please apply c/o The Principal, The Lady Marchmoor Finishing School for Graceful Deportment and Etiquette.

DIRTY rotten scheming male chauvinistic two-timing thug, wishes to meet brash tarty sleep-around flirty woman ... with a view to possible employment in a television soap opera.

LOST, Thursday — halfway up A1 — virginity — please ring Judy and ask to speak to the midwife.

SCREW drivers? We do! Ring Babs and Sandra. No appointments necessary. OAPs half price.

AMBITIOUS young film director, at present working on full-length feature would like to meet woman from the props department who can offer him support.

MALE bridge player would like to meet lady bridge player with a view to sharing a few rubbers.

83-YEAR-OLD nymphomaniac woman with rapidly failing eyesight would like to make acquaintance of the tall thin silent gentleman with a lampshade on his head who tried to seduce her in the corner of her own living-room.

MASOCHISTIC man wishes to meet sadistic woman who can show him the ropes.

CHELSEA supporter, into kicking, biting, spitting, would like to form meaningful, sincere relationship with a large piece of reinforced concrete. Alternatively would like to meet anyone interested in playing head tennis with a live hand grenade.

MAGICO, the amazing disappearing man, would like to form ...

I AM the world's most sensual man. I am incredible in bed. I have been making love continuously since I was fifteen and am now the world's finest lover. Now, twenty years later, I would like to see what it feels like when there's someone else with me.

'O'-LEVEL examiner would like to form stable, caring relationship with a warm loving woman. Discuss.

MALE crossword compiler would like to meet female crossword compiler with a view to a good old type of rough coarse pipe tobacco (four letters).

POLITICIAN who must remain anonymous seeks discreet affair with intimate person who must promise not to tell Denis.

NEWSPAPER journalist would like to meet curvy curvaceous lustful lovelies with a view to sexy sexy sexy naughty antics of the love-crazed sex frolics, probe. Contact the Editor, *Financial Times*.

Australian men

BY AUSTRALIAN WOMEN

'The first Australian man I went out with ... I asked him to do something to knock me off my feet, so he stood behind me and broke wind.'

'His idea of foreplay was a burp.'

'He was kind. He once bought me a sheepskin coat. The only trouble was the sheep was still wearing it.'

'He was into serious drinking ... I mean he went on the wagon for a week and Castlemaine had to close down three breweries.'

'He had a gut the size of Ayers Rock ... when we made love I used to have to use a pair of step-ladders to get into position.'

'Unkempt? I remember he once cleaned out the fluff from inside his navel and for three days I thought it was a new hearth rug.'

'His socks were so high the drugs squad once busted them for possession.'

This page taken from the *Australian Kama Sutra* (in fact this page forms the *Complete Australian Kama Sutra*).

THE ACT
OF UNION

Just like any unionist, having paid your dues you will expect to see a return, and in this case the return comes in the form of THE ACT OF UNION:

Intercourse techniques

GOOD   BAD

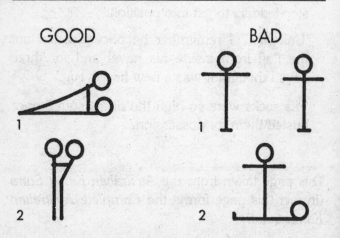

GOOD   BAD

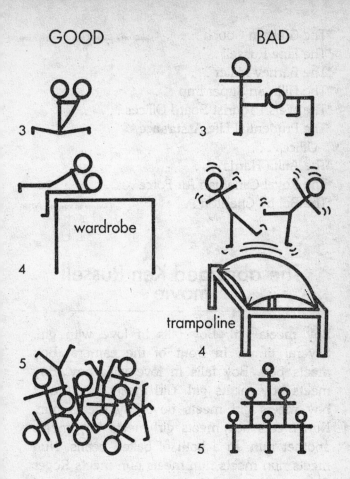

3   3

4
wardrobe

                                        4
                                        trampoline

5

                                        5

***** NEW !!!!!

During preparation of this book a number of
brand-new love making positions became
known. Overleaf is the authoritative list of new
positions:

*The Graham Gooch . . . (details not available at time of going to press)
*The Jane Russell . . . ''
*The Barney Miller . . . ''
*The Hillman Super Imp . . . ,,
*The Welsh Tourist Board Offices . . . ,,
*The Prudential Life Assurance
    Offices . . . ''
*The Anita Harris . . . ,,
*The Royal Canadian Air Force . . . ,,
*The Bobby Charlton . . . (deleted on legal advice — Ed)

The abridged Ken Russell movie

Boy meets girl. Boy falls in love with girl. Several times. In front of the camera. Boy meets boy. Boy falls in love with boy. Boy meets boy meets girl. Girl meets boy meets boy meets girl meets boy. Boy meets nun. Nun meets boy meets girl meets boy meets another nun. In a bath of baked beans. Nun meets nun meets nun meets nun meets Roger Daltrey. With no clothes on. Girl meets girl meets girl meets girl meets girl meets girl meets Roger Daltrey. With nun's clothing on. The end.

Reprinted from *The Ken Russell Guide to Movie-making*

7

ADVANCED PRACTICES

Having mastered the fundamentals of sex you will soon find yourself looking forward to more advanced practices. This will give you added pleasure and ensure your sex life does not become boring. Here are the top suggestions for advancing your performance in the libido stakes:

1. *New positions.* Numerous books exist detailing new and exciting positions that can be tried for added stimulation. Do not confuse these with yoga or martial arts manuals which may look similar to the novice but which could induce quite horrific injuries if employed in error.

2. *Different times.* Try making love at different times of the day. Mid-morning, lunch time, over breakfast (note: if making love over the breakfast table do ensure all breakfast

things have been cleared away first. There are few more uncomfortable things in life than making love with a salt cruet and half a jar of marmalade sticking out of your back).

3. *Eroticism.* One of the latest stimulants that couples have found useful is the video camera. Filming your performance before the camera then playing the results back afterwards can be very erotic indeed. Always use a static camera and a 120 or 180 cassette. There is little fun in having your partner wander round, camera in hand, looking for that perfect close-up shot. Nor is it much fun embarking on your home movie career only to discover the tape has run out at the vital moment leaving you to repeat the whole thing for a second time. Above all else ensure the tape is not left lying around. Imagine the shock of inviting your neighbours round to watch your latest loan from the video shop only to then recoil in horror as your intimate sexual details are revealed upon the screen.

4. *Sado-masochism.* Rubbery, bondage and leatherwear are all acceptable forms of stimulation. Not included are full chain mail, sealed lead body caskets, and the entire

contents of the Tower of London torture gallery.

5. *Mirrors.* Wall mirrors, ceiling mirrors, floor mirrors and concealed mirrors are all used to spice up your yearnings. Take care when using mirrors. There is a risk of complete disorientation and you may end up making love to a non-existent image of your real partner.

8
THE KAMA SUTRA ORIGAMI BOOK

The secrets of the *Kama Sutra Origami Book* have been locked away for centuries. Now that secret is out as we publish a page from that most passionate of books. Simply fold along the dotted lines as indicated and unlock the erotic secrets of the East.

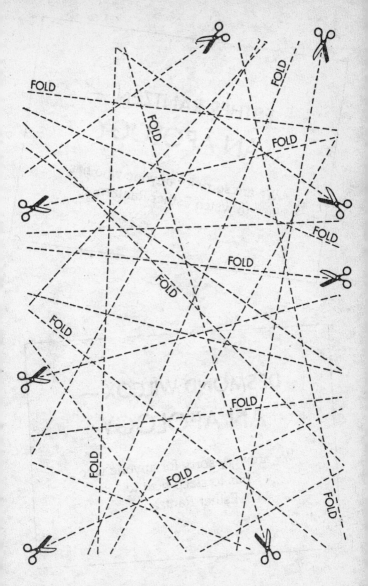

ESTHER RANTZEN —
AN APOLOGY

We are sorry for anyone who has
to watch Esther Rantzen.

DESMOND WILCOX —
AN APOLOGY

We are very sorry for anyone who
has to sleep next to
Esther Rantzen.

POST-MATCH TACTICS

Learn to perfect your post-play, the post-coital equivalent of foreplay. How to respond after making the beast with two backs. What to do, what not to do. Don't upset your partner by sitting up straightaway afterwards to finish *The Times* crossword. Don't use the bedside phone to ring up your best friend and tell him what it was like ... !!!

Things to do after sexual intercourse

Good things:

Nothing
Sleep
Smoke a cigarette

Smoke another cigarette
Say, 'How was it for you?'

Bad things:

Ask your partner what their name is
Phone up a friend and tell them how it was
Laugh hysterically
Fart hysterically
Smoke a pipe
Listen to a piece of brass band music
Whistle tunelessly
Take your teeth out
Read a copy of *Exchange and Mart*
Say, 'Is that it, then?'

WHAT THE IRISH
CENSOR SAW

So often in erotic publications the all-important vital bits are concealed behind the blackout marks of the public censor's pencil. Now we have collected together all those many erotic pieces and publish them for the first time in this ... the uncensored file!!!

What the Irish censor saw

AN APPEAL

Republished from *47 Ways to Lose Your Sexual Appetite* (volume 93)

An appeal

Good evening.

I'd like to take this opportunity to appeal to you all honestly, openly and sincerely on behalf of a group of people who desperately need your help. I am talking, as I'm sure you know, about holiday-makers who have to sit on the beach in summer watching middle-aged women with droopy boobs wobbling across the sand in bikini tops that don't fit.

You know every year hundreds and hundreds of poor innocent holiday-makers have their holidays spoilt by the sight of paunchy fat tarts running round the beach, their nasty loose bristols straining at the leash like a couple of Jack Russells on heat. And you know each year it gets worse. More and more shapeless women are wobbling their way onto our beaches in groaning swimwear, putting the donkeys off their food and leaving pot holes big enough for a man to fall down wherever they lie face down on the sand.

Take this exciting hand-crocheted woman's bikini in exciting King Edward potato style. This bikini top was removed from a lady bather only this morning by the tide. And by a large Army bulldozer. And now that the fat floozie to whom this brassiere belongs has taken her plump ploppies off the beach it is safe for ordinary decent bathers to enjoy.

And you know our work doesn't just end there. We aim to rid our beaches of those funny rubber bathing caps with yellow flowers on top and a chin strap missing underneath as well! After all, what could be more upsetting as you shelter from a force nine gale behind a flimsy wind break than to see a great fat flabby tart with a baggy backside and bristols down to her knees racing head first towards you down the beach like a runaway Duncan Goodhew with mammary implants?

What can you do to help?

Well, this year the ROYAL SOCIETY FOR THE PREVENTION OF FLABBY FAT TARTS RUNNING ROUND OUR BEACHES IN OUT OF SHAPE OUT OF DATE OUT OF ONE CUP BIKINIS are launching a campaign to draw attention to the distress these women cause. This distinctive sign, DON'T GO NEAR THE WATER YOU OLD BAG OR YOU MIGHT GET HARPOONED BY A PASSING JAPANESE WHALING SHIP BY MISTAKE is now available. As too is this attractive six foot high cardboard box which fits neatly over any big busty substance ruining your hols.

Remember, podgy fat plumpies with two bowls of pink porridge swimming around on their chests are a serious threat to our holiday fun.

Help us to help yourself.

Tell your mum to stay at home this year.

12

PERFORMANCE

Like any budding professional you should start to measure your performance. This simple questionnaire lets you see your performance improving screw-by-screw.

Don't ask your partner to fill in the questionnaire immediately after sex!

	Marks out of Ten		
	Bad		Good

Does your partner remove
their clothes before
commencing?
Yes = Good, No = Bad   1 2 3 4 5 6 7 8 9 10

Does your partner remove
their bobble hat before
commencing?
Yes = Good, No = Bad   1 2 3 4 5 6 7 8 9 10

Does your partner remove
your bobble hat before
commencing?
Yes = Good, No = Bad   1 2 3 4 5 6 7 8 9 10

Does your partner ask your
name before commencing?   1 2 3 4 5 6 7 8 9 10
Yes = Good, No = Bad

Does your partner wear a
blindfold?   1 2 3 4 5 6 7 8 9 10
Yes = Bad, No = Good

Does your partner eat a
sandwich during foreplay?   1 2 3 4 5 6 7 8 9 10
Yes = Bad, No = Good

Does your partner watch
television while you are
performing?   1 2 3 4 5 6 7 8 9 10
Yes = Bad, No = Good

Does your partner break wind
during any act of love making? 1 2 3 4 5 6 7 8 9 10
Yes = Bad, No = Good

Does your partner laugh when
you suggest you try again? 1 2 3 4 5 6 7 8 9 10
Yes = Bad, No = Good

Does your partner use a stop
watch to time the
performance?   1 2 3 4 5 6 7 8 9 10
Yes = Bad, No = Good

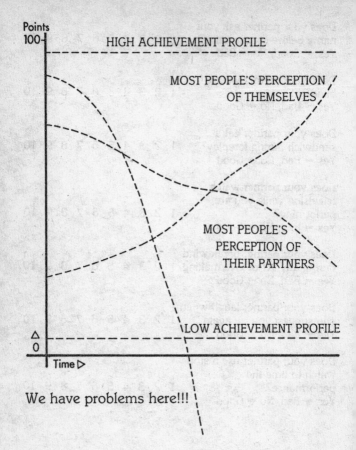

Points
100-

HIGH ACHIEVEMENT PROFILE

MOST PEOPLE'S PERCEPTION
OF THEMSELVES

MOST PEOPLE'S
PERCEPTION OF
THEIR PARTNERS

LOW ACHIEVEMENT PROFILE

Time ▷

We have problems here!!!

WHAT TO DO IF ...?

Even the best of lovers run into problems occasionally. Reduce the risk of embarrassment with this simple-to-use fault-finder section. Printed in especially bold text it is especially suitable for discriminating torchlight reading.

I experience a rush of blood to the head followed by a sudden feeling of impending darkness
YOUR CAMP BED HAS JUST FOLDED UP WITH YOU INSIDE IT.

I experience a hot flush to the loins followed by a wet sensation on the bed linen
YOU HAVE ROLLED ON TOP OF THE HOT-WATER BOTTLE AND BURST IT.

My partner seems strangely
lifeless and fails to respond
to my amorous advances
CHECK TO ENSURE SHE IS
STILL FULLY INFLATED.

When we make love I feel a
violent sensation on the
head and am gripped by the
sound of a thousand guns
going off inside my head
LUCKY YOU

I have great difficulty
performing when I make love
and my manhood seems
strangely elusive to find
CHECK THAT YOU ARE NOT
STILL WEARING YOUR
UNDERPANTS.

I experience a sudden loss of
sensuality accompanied by a
feeling of cold pain rising
in the buttocks and lower
back
CHECK THAT YOU HAVEN'T
FALLEN OUT OF BED AGAIN.

I feel a cold sensation
around my neck and a
sharpness across my face
CHECK YOU HAVEN'T
KNOCKED YOUR DENTURE
GLASS OVER OR THAT THE
TEETH HAVEN'T ATTACHED
THEMSELVES TO YOUR NOSE.

I have a sensation as if I'm
floating followed by a
terrible, dull throbbing pain
in my head
CHECK THAT YOU HAVEN'T
FALLEN OUT OF THE TOP
DECK OF A SET OF BUNK
BEDS.

I experience a sudden
stabbing pain to my left knee
and a sharp sensation to the
middle of my back and my
right arm becomes locked in
position
TRY USING THE BACK SEAT
INSTEAD!

And here are some answers from the *Irish Perfumed Garden*'s special agony aunt, 'County' Claire.

Dear Claire,

Hello, luvvies, Claire here again answering more of your questions. And we start with Mary from Ballybunion. Hello Mary luvvie. Are you listening, acushla? Mary asks ... Dear Claire — what d'you recommend for a large stain in the middle of a table cloth? Well, Mary we've given the matter a lot of thought and we recommend beetroot! That gives the best stain of all.

Mick next. Hello Mick. Mick writes ... Dear Claire — my wife's left me, my children have run away from home, I've lost my job, crashed my car, defaulted on my mortgage, fallen into debt, started drinking, and become a hopeless, homeless derelict wreck ... is there anything I can do? Well, yes, Mick there is something you can do ... you can stop writing these nasty horrible letters to me, they're just so terribly depressing.

Kate now. Hello Kate luvvie darling pet. Kate writes ... I am twenty-one and my boyfriend is ninety-eight and has invited me on a dirty weekend away and I want to know if there is anything I can buy him as a present afterwards. Well, yes Kate luvvie, there is something you can get him ... a wreath!

Kitty has written to me from Killarney. Hello Kitty luvvie in Killarney. Kitty wants to know the answer to a very personal question ... well Kitty the answer to your very personal question is no, you can't get pregnant like that, but you can have an awful lot of fun trying.

Delia next. Hello Delia pet luvvie darling. Delia has written to say ... Dear Claire, my husband is a beast in bed, he treats me like his slave and makes me do all sorts of things I don't want to ... is there anything at all I can do? Well, yes, of course there is something you can do, Delia ... you can hand him my phone number and tell him to give me a call any time.

And finally, luvvies, I've got one last letter and it's from Catherine in Connemara ... Hello Catherine luvvie ... well, Catherine I've read your letter — several times — and the answers to the various questions you raise are:
1. Yes
2. Every alternative Saturday
3. A large grapefruit
... but then again Catherine ... don't let what I do influence you in any way!!!

14

THE
A TO Z OF
CARNAL KNOWLEDGE

Is premature ejaculation a form of speaking before you're spoken to. The answer to this and many other questions are to be found below in the A to Z of Carnal Knowledge.

A Aphrodisiac

Substance given to increase sexual desires and put potency back into your potency. Typical examples of aphrodisiacs are oysters. But ask yourself this ... if oysters are such a turn-on why have you never seen an oyster as the centre spread in *Penthouse*?

B Bums/Boobs/Breasts/Botties/Bouncies/Brassiere/Beaver/etc. ...

Over 50% of sexually relatable words begin with the letter 'B'. If a sexual word is required chances are this is the letter under which to find it.

CAUTION: Not all words beginning with 'B' have sexual implications, for example:

Bungalow
Bread board
Baroness Summerskill*
Biggles
Biscuit barrel
Belch
Burp
Bedbug
Bank manager
Bagpipes

* Occasionally used as a term of arousal in Hungary

C Crumpet merchant

Referential term used to imply men of great sexual prowess. Not to be confused with Muffinman which is the name given to a sexual deviant who performs certain unnatural acts with particular types of donkeys.

D Dirty Movies

The World's Top Ten Porno Pix!!!

1. NAUGHTY NYMPHO NIGHT NURSES ON THE JOB

2. SAUCY SECRETS OF SEXY SINFUL SUSIE

3. RED HOT PASSIONS OF A TYPEWRITER REPAIR MAN FROM WEXFORD

4. LURID LUSTS OF AN OUT-OF-WORK CHIROPODIST WITH A FLAT IN MAGILLYCUDDY'S REEKS

5. CONFESSIONS OF A PORNO ANTIQUARIAN BOOKSELLER FROM A VILLAGE JUST OUTSIDE CASTLEFERGIS

6. TORRID NIGHTS OF A SWEDISH OBSTETRICIAN IN A LARGE DUBLIN TEACHING HOSPITAL

7. SEXY ANTICS OF A SEX HUNGRY PERSON AGED 35-40, MEDIUM BUILD, FAIR COMPLEXION, LAST SEEN WEARING A FAWN-COLOURED ANORAK AND NAVY BLUE TROUSERS

8. SEXPLOITS OF A SENIOR CAVITY WALL INSULATION TECHNOLOGIST NOW LIVING IN BALLYJAMESDUFF AND COVERING THE ROSCOMMON DISTRICT FRANCHISE FOR AN AMERICAN BASED COMPANY WITH OFFICES THROUGHOUT THE REPUBLIC

9. AMOROUS NIGHTS OF THE LOVE-HUNGRY STICK INSECT

10. I WAS THE MAN WHO THOUGHT UP THE TITLES TO ALL THE PORNO MOVIES EVER SEEN AND THEN I RAN OUT OF IDEAS!!!

E Erection

Not to be confused with an election which is a system of allocating power by means of a vote. Except in China where an erection is a system of voting, and an election ... well, let's just say that explaining to a Chinaman that the people of Britain hold an election once every five years is not the easiest of tasks.

F Foreplay

Name given to any act taking place before sex. Normally reserved to obvious sexual-type behaviour. If you put the cat out immediately before having sex then this would not normally be called foreplay.

G G-string

Type of undergarment worn to reveal male contours. Takes its name from G-sharp which is the note most men tend to reach when wearing such a garment.

H Keith HARRIS and Orville

Name given to a sexual act which involves placing one's hand up inside a duck's bum.

I Intercourse

Another name given to the sex act much used by television doctors.

J Jellies and Creams

Often used as lubricants during sex. Do not confuse with jelly-and-ice-cream which should never be used and especially not whilst being eaten.

K Kinky Underwear

Often worn to arouse and stimulate a partner. Kinky underwear comprises brassieres, split-crotch panties, suspender belts, corsets, negligees, and fishnet stockings. And the women usually wear the same as well.

L Love Nest

Type of abode much fancied by Fleet Street commentators and implying some form of ornithologically-related retreat with feathers and twigs and *BIRDS* !

M Maze

Use this unique Irish maze as a prelude to any sexual activity:

Start here

Finish here

73

N Nipples

Also Nipples/Nippy Nips/Nip Nips etc. Sensual buds found on the chest and usually appearing in pairs. Where fifty or more nipples appear on the chest check for the presence of chickenpox. Not to be confused with Naples — which is an Italian town, and Nibbles which are light snacks eaten between meals.

O Oral Sex

When you just talk about it.
Also: Oral Contraception — when you talk your way out of it.

P Permissive

Woman who walks around with a four-poster bed strapped to her back.

Q Queue

Line that forms outside Vicki Hodge's bedroom.

R Religion

Tracey?
Sharron?
Sheila?
Mandy?
Babs?

Dawn?
Penelope?
Sindy?
Samantha?
Amanda?
Maureen?
Cheryl?
Brenda?
Janice?
Hilda?
Annabelle?
Deidre?
Mavis?
Prudence?
Vera?
... and if it's a boy?
... we'll call him ... Jesus!!!

S Sun

TELEX ATTN SUN GROUP NEWSPAPERS

ADVERTISING COPY

PLEASE ENSURE FOLLOWING COPY IS
USED IN THIS WEEK'S SUN NEWSPAPER
ADVERTS ON TELEVISION:

NEXT WEEK AND ALL NEXT WEEK IN THE
SUN ... NEXT WEEK AND ALL NEXT WEEK
WE'VE GOT THE SEXY SINFUL SECRETS OF
THE COUNTRY'S SEXIEST LOVERS ...

THE SAUCY SEXPOT RAVE-UP
REVELATIONS OF OUR RAUNCHY RANDY
RED-HOT READERS ... YES, NEXT WEEK
AND ALL NEXT WEEK IT'S INTERCOURSE
WEEK IN THE SEXY SIZZLING SUN ...
EVERY DAY YOUR SEXY SIZZLING
SUNSATIONAL SUN BRINGS YOU ALL THE
SEXUAL INTERCOURSE STORIES AND
MORE ... NEXT WEEK IS SEXY SIZZLING
COPULATING PENIS-ERECTING
VAGINAL-ENTERING SEMEN-
EJACULATING INTERCOURSE WEEK IN
THE SUN ... YOU CAN'T BEAT YOUR
FORNICATING SUN.

REPEAT THIS IS THE COPY FOR ALL SUN
TV ADS

YOURS

RUPERT

T Tunnel of Love (See opposite).

U Eunuch

Person of indeterminate sex including male
airline stewards, female tennis players, and BBC
wardrobe assistants.

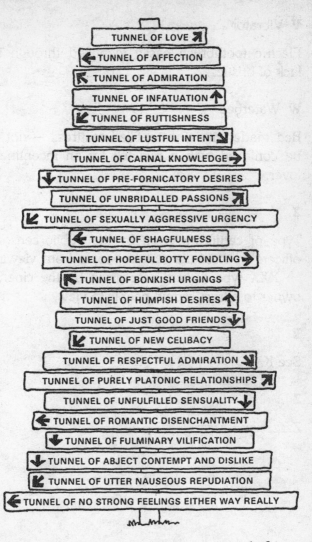

TUNNEL OF LOVE ↗

← TUNNEL OF AFFECTION

↖ TUNNEL OF ADMIRATION

TUNNEL OF INFATUATION ↑

↙ TUNNEL OF RUTTISHNESS

TUNNEL OF LUSTFUL INTENT ↘

TUNNEL OF CARNAL KNOWLEDGE →

↓ TUNNEL OF PRE-FORNICATORY DESIRES

TUNNEL OF UNBRIDALLED PASSIONS ↗

↙ TUNNEL OF SEXUALLY AGGRESSIVE URGENCY

← TUNNEL OF SHAGFULNESS

TUNNEL OF HOPEFUL BOTTY FONDLING →

↖ TUNNEL OF BONKISH URGINGS

TUNNEL OF HUMPISH DESIRES ↑

TUNNEL OF JUST GOOD FRIENDS ↓

↙ TUNNEL OF NEW CELIBACY

TUNNEL OF RESPECTFUL ADMIRATION ↘

TUNNEL OF PURELY PLATONIC RELATIONSHIPS ↗

TUNNEL OF UNFULFILLED SENSUALITY ↓

← TUNNEL OF ROMANTIC DISENCHANTMENT

↓ TUNNEL OF FULMINARY VILIFICATION

↓ TUNNEL OF ABJECT CONTEMPT AND DISLIKE

↙ TUNNEL OF UTTER NAUSEOUS REPUDIATION

← TUNNEL OF NO STRONG FEELINGS EITHER WAY REALLY

Example of a very comprehensive tunnel of love !!!!!

V Vibrator

Electric toothbrush easily identified through its lack of bristles.

W Waterbed

Bed made with a water-filled mattress — not to be confused with a bed left by an incontinent lover.

X

Type of certificate given by the public censor's officers to dissuade certain people from viewing ... XXX type of certificate given by the cinema owner to attract certain people to view.

Y

See K.

Z

Zzzzzzzzzzzzzzz.

15
THE CARNAL KNOWLEDGE PHRASE BOOK

Top Ten chat-up lines

- 'Did I screw you last night?'

- 'How much?'

- '*How much ?!*'

- 'I love you. Now drop your knickers.'

- 'Look, there's another couple of hours but if I don't find anyone else then you'll do.'

- 'I've always found you attractive, ever since I went to school with your grandchildren.'

- 'Do you always wear your pants round your ankles?'

- 'I love it when you smile. It reminds me of my job as a crash investigator for an insurance firm.'

- 'I don't treat women like sex objects; now strap this mattress to your back.'

- 'Meet me on top of the wardrobe in five minutes' time.'

Irish universities' examination paper

'O'-LEVEL SEX ORAL

MULTIPLE CHOICE

QUESTION 1

Here darlin', d'you fancy it tonight?
(Answer *YES* or *NO*.)

THE END

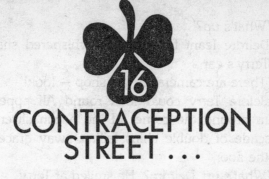

16
CONTRACEPTION STREET ...

'Hello Alf, hello Deirdre ...' Terry Duckworth walked manfully into Alf's shop at the end of Contraception Street.

'Hello, lad,' smiled Alf, groaning under the weight of a huge bag of potatoes that turned out to be his stomach.

'What can we do for you, Terry?' smiled Deirdre running a spare grease-gun through her hair.

'Just a packet of contraceptives please, Deirdre,' replied Terry, putting a pound coin down on the counter.

Deirdre paused for a second.

'You what, Terry lad ...?'

Terry smiled confidently.

'A packet of contraceptives please, Deirdre luv,' and he pushed the coin across the counter towards Deirdre as payment.

Deirdre coloured instantly.

'Shhhh Terry ...'

Terry seemed surprised.

81

'What's up?'

Deirdre leant forward and whispered sharply in Terry's ear:

'There are cameras in the shop — look!'

Before Terry could look round Alf appeared from around the corner of the bacon slicer, his cascade of double chins falling away gracefully to the floor.

'What's up, Deirdre?' He smiled at Terry.

'It's Terry, Alf ...' Deirdre nodded across to where Terry stood, 'he wants a packet of Durex.'

Alf froze.

'You want what, lad?'

Terry smiled.

'A packet of rubbers please, Alf.'

Alf could feel a surge of temper that ran up his neck and caused him to tremble.

'Are you trying to be funny, lad?'

Terry seemed hurt.

'No, Alf,' he sounded genuinely pained. 'If I'd wanted to be funny I'd have had my hair cut by the same person who cuts Deirdre's.'

Alf steadied himself.

'You're trying to get this shop a bad name aren't you lad!'

Terry raised his hands in disbelief.

'No, Alf of course I'm not.'

Alf seemed uncertain.

'Then what d'you have to come in here asking for ...' he opened his mouth and mouthed the words 'a packet of Durex' silently.

Terry smiled confidently.

'You stock them don't you ... you're a shop?'

Alf raised himself to his full height — three foot eight inches — and scowled.

'No!'

Terry paused for a second.

'Yes, you do.'

Alf's frown deepened.

'No, we don't.'

Terry eyed him with a stare and leant over.

'Then what are these then?' and he pulled a packet of Durex Featherlight from under the counter.

Alf leapt forward at once and smacked the packet from Terry's grip.

'Put those away!'

Terry bent down to pick the packet up.

'What, these you mean?'

Deirdre reached over and grabbed Terry by the arm.

'Put those away Terry, there's cameras in the shop!'

Terry seemed pensive, troubled, his lip curled in defiance and he turned square on to Deirdre.

'Oh I see, I get it ...' he spat the words out as he spoke 'it's all right for me to have been seen to have got a girl pregnant on screen but it's not all right for me to have been seen to have learnt my lesson and to now be taking all the necessary precautions.'

Alf intervened.

'Look, have a packet of biscuits on the house instead,' and he thrust a packet of milk chocolate digestives into Terry's hand.

Terry threw the biscuits down and kicked them to one side.

'I don't want biscuits! I want a packet of Durex! This is a shop isn't it? Shops sell Durex ... well, why can't I come in here and buy a packet of Durex like in any normal shop ... why must I always buy biscuits or tea or packets of cornflakes or something like that? How are cornflakes going to stop me getting a girl pregnant?'

'Well, if you sprinkle them on the bed beforehand you certainly won't feel much like making love with them crunching away underneath you!' smirked Deirdre.

Terry smashed his fist down on the counter.

'I'm not much interested in what you and Ken do to stop having babies!' and he jabbed his finger menacingly at Deirdre's eye.

'Here, have this lad.'

It was Alf who intervened.

'Australian lager — take it — take it — better than any contraceptive ...'

Terry looked on blankly.

'You what?'

Alf grinned again.

'Better than any contraceptive on the market lad.'

Terry looked at the cans of lager.

'How d'you work that out, fatman?'

Alf smiled confidently.

'Well, drink half a dozen cans of that lad and there's no way you'll be able to get a girl pregnant.'

Terry paused, then changed his tone.

'Deirdre — you're a woman — just — you understand about these sorts of things — look, all I want is a packet of Durex.'

Alf turned on Deirdre.

'Don't listen to him Deirdre ...!' And he turned to stand with his back to the camera, blocking out the view and humming loudly.

'A packet of Durex please Deirdre.' Terry tried shouting above the noise.

'La la i la la la laa li laa la la ...'

Terry tried again.

'A packet of Durex please Deirdre ...'

'La la la li laa laa la li laa la li ...'

Louder and louder grew Terry's shouts. Louder and louder grew Alf's singing and behind Alf's back could just be seen the upraised fists of Deirdre Barlow as she thumped and pushed Terry back out into the street where he stood banging and hammering on the shop window. Deirdre gave a sigh.

'It's all right Alf, he's gone now ...'

'La la li laa ... oh, has he?'

Alf looked round and checked.

'That boy will give this shop a bad name Deirdre.' Alf ran a finger across his brow to mop away the sweat. 'You mark my words if he doesn't!'

Deirdre started to clear up the mess and gave a shrug.

'Aye well I've got rid of him, Alf, so let's forget all about it shall we ...?'

Alf nodded.

'He comes in here deliberately to disrupt the unreal calm of the street with its strangely biopic charm that regards the male condom as in some way taboo whilst regarding the result of sexual liaison as a rich picking ground for script and storyline treatments ... he should know by now that we depend on an uneasy truce between reality and fiction to maintain the strangely uneasy charm of our fictional world.'

Deirdre nodded. She'd heard it all a hundred times before.

'Yes Alf I know ... now let's not talk about it ... all right?'

Alf lifted his three stomachs onto the top of the counter and smiled.

'Agreed, Deirdre,' he laughed, 'the less said the better!'

Deirdre nodded.

'We can do without interruptions like that,' she sighed.

Alf shook his head.

'You can say that again Deirdre.'

Deirdre frowned and looked up from the order book that she had been reading.

'Oh, by the way Alf ...'

Alf took the pencil out of his mouth and cupped an ear.

'Yes?'

Deirdre pointed to the book.

'I nearly forgot ... you'll need to order some more naughty French ticklers ... Hilda Ogden bought the last one this morning!!!!'

BIBLIOGRAPHY

The author of *The Irish Perfumed Garden* would like to register his thanks to the following publications which were used extensively in the preparation of the text.

1. *How To Make Love In An Expensive Yachting Marina*

2. *How To Make Love In An Expensive Morris Marina*

3. *How to Make Love In An Expensive Kensington Wine Bar (Without Detection)*

4. *How To Make Love In An Expensive Kensington Wine Bar (With Detection)*

5. *The Royal Book of Nookie*

6. *The Reader's Digest Book Of The Fondle*

7. *The Country Diary Of An Edwardian Lady Nympho Cookbook*

8. *The Boys' Own Book Of the Boys' Own*

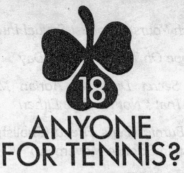

18

ANYONE FOR TENNIS?

A salutory story on the morals of sex and sport.

No sex please we're British tennis players

'So you want to be tennis stars, do you?'

The coach held his racket close to his chest and caught his new charges with a fixed stare. They shuffled uneasily from foot to foot and mumbled their agreement. The coach ran his racket through his hands a few times and paused.

'All right, well what's the first thing you need if you want to become a tennis star?'

His voice barked out across the empty courts. There was silence as the youngsters plucked up courage to answer.

'A nationality other than British?'

The young voice sounded uncertain as it spoke.

'A funny foreign name?'

The coach brought his racket down swiftly on the net cord and barked angrily:

'The first thing you need if you're to become a tennis star is absolute obedience to the basic law of tennis stardom and that law says quite simply that if you're going to win at tennis then you can say goodbye to this.'

And he patted himself lightly on the crutch. The youngsters shuffled their feet again.

'Pardon, sir?'

The coach drew his racket back and tapped it against his crutch.

'No nookie, lad — start knobbing around and you're finished as a tennis player! Look at McEnroe — off the girlies he's unbeatable ... starts to mess around with that Tatum floozie and his tennis career's gone down the Swannee ... or Borg!!! Soon as he got the hots for those women he could kiss his Grand Slam chances goodbye!'

The youngsters looked around thinking that there might be something to say. At last a voice piped up from the back.

'And that's all there is to becoming an International Tennis player is it, sir? No naughties?'

The coach straightened his back and tapped the side of his nose knowingly.

'That's right lad! Look at Becker — no girl-friend — he's unbeatable! We don't need special training camps ... plenty of clean thoughts and a hefty hump to humping and we've as good as won Wimbledon!'

He stopped to draw breath.

'What about woman players, sir?'

The voice quivered as it spoke.

'Same applies ... Navratilova — would you give her one? Not a chance! Ugly as an ox ... that's why she's a champ! Billie Jean King ... Virginia Wade ... it's easy ... work it out for yourself ... why are all the top women players ugly? Answer — because ugly women don't stay up half the night having nookie!!!'

'Chris Lloyd isn't ugly, sir!'

The voice of protest came from a fresh-faced hopeful at the front of the young players. The coach leant forward, his racket ready to cuff the young lad if he spoke out of turn again.

'What did you say, lad?'

The youngster swallowed hard.

'Chris Lloyd isn't ugly, sir ... but she's still a champ.'

The coach drew back.

'No, but there's a reason for that ...'

They waited for him to continue.

'Yes, sir?'

He saw their eager faces looking up at him and took them in with a sincere glance.

'Well, it's obvious, isn't it?' He ran his racket down his leg as he spoke, '... I mean, would you want to have nookie with a husband who is prettier than you?'

There was a moment's silence while the remark sunk in. Then the youngsters seemed content.

'Right, everyone?'

The coach's voice sang out across the court.

'Sixty pages of Wisden batting averages before lunch and no impure thoughts!!!'

19
THE EMERALD GIGOLO

A Short Story

He was poor and old. His clothes were the coarse rough sacking of the poorest peasant. He drove only the thinnest goats to market ... but beneath this façade he was ... *the highest paid gigolo in the Emerald Isle.*

Patrick O'Hennessey lived alone. Save, that were, for his goats. For ninety-seven years he had toiled alone — night and day — to raise a paltry income that was barely enough to support him.

His farm — a few rough acres and a small stone billet — lay high above the town in a steep valley that few other men seldom visited. Here he carved out a meagre existence from soils that would break the plough and turn themselves only to the poorest grass.

Patrick rarely visited the town now, once a month maybe, to pick up provisions and sell the odd goat. It was a long way down the valley and his frail legs were no longer able to support him; the right one had got dry rot and badly needed replacing though where a poor peasant could afford new wood was uncertain.

Which was why he was up early for today's long walk into town. At ten o'clock with the sun high up in the sky Patrick reached the outskirts of Bollocks — the small market town where for thirteen years he had lived as a boy (he had in fact been thirty-eight at the time but he had lived as a boy; attending school daily and joining in the children's games).

There were few people about as he crossed the courtyard in front of the small wooden door that served as the town's main gate. Most would be at work in the fields that gathered round the town in thick green patchwork.

The old, narrow streets that wound their way up steadily from the small market square were half-clad in dark shadows to which Patrick stayed close as he picked his way down into the square.

A woman — a woman in dark robes — passed quickly and was gone. Another appeared for a brief second at a half-shuttered window. Bollocks had many such women.

Slowly now, his feet sore and blistered from the dusty roads, Patrick edged his way along the north side of the square — past a small group of workmen deep in conversation by Mackilli-krankies bar. Past where the brothers O'Toole were playing chess. And up towards the one shop that served for all the town.

The shop was empty — no one did business at this time. The hour was too early. Patrick wiped his brow with a threadbare rag that had once been red and waited for the old widow to enter from her room at the back. It was quiet; the widow had clearly not heard him for she was still snoring. Patrick coughed and shuffled his tired feet on the dusty floor. The widow stirred.

She was large — her body nearly filling the small space from which she dealt with all her customers. She slackened the buckle on the cheap belt that held her filthy black skirt round her broad hips; 'Yes?'

Patrick handed her a card. Dirty and bent, it bore the efforts of many hour's work:

92-year-old gigolo available at competitive rates. Hourly, daily, weekly terms. Reduced charges for pensioners ...

... Also soured goat milk cheese for sale by the sockfull.

Apply: Patrick O'Hennessey.

The widow read it slowly then lifted down a small cork board from the window and slipped it into a small space in the top corner,

'Fifteen pence in advance!'

It was late when Patrick eventually returned home that evening. He put the goats to bed and was about to turn in himself when there came a faint knock at the door. Shuffling across the bare stone floor, he tied his wig back on with a large untidy bow beneath his chin and unbolted the door ...

'I've come, Patrick.' It was the late Dermot O'Growbag's wife. Aged eighty-seven. It was eleven o'clock.

Patrick's goats didn't get fed till after noon next day.

The next evening Patrick was resting, for he was no longer the young man he had once been. The sun had gone down. A small fire glowed gently in the grate. There was again a sound at the door, a knock. He stirred himself from his slumbers and again removed the latch. It was the very late peat digger's wife, Mary O'Rourke, two years the right side of 103.

That next day the goats didn't get fed till mid-afternoon.

Patrick took a brief limp round the fields. He was asleep in the front room when a knock on the door sounded at half-past four. It was the widow O'Malley.

Patrick screwed his leg back on and hobbled across the uneven floor, pausing to pick up his glass eye from the dish of polish in which it had been soaking.

The next day the goats had to feed themselves. Patrick had barely the energy left to see how his acres were.

By the middle of the next week Patrick had seen thirty-four different widows and had barely chance to rise from bed each day for more than a couple of hours.

Already he was booked solid till mid-November. He introduced matinees on Wednesdays and Saturdays and early evening performances on Tuesdays and Thursdays.

He owned the best goat-cheese press in County Kerry. There was a gold-plated goat in the shed outside, and a goat's milk bed in the end room. He had a goat in Monte Carlo, and another in Los Angeles. He owned an engraved set of the finest ebony wooden legs. And 200 different glass eyes. His wigs were from Savile Row, the bows that tied them — silk. He was the highest paid gigolo in Ireland!

There was a knock at the door; it was the widow Shaunessy. Patrick cleared his new goats from the bedroom and locked the door. The next day the servants fed the goats.

Patrick could have anything he wanted. At 97 he at last had riches. Riches he would never have known had he not placed that advert with the widow in the shop. And yet …?

And yet was he not now less happy than when he had been poor? Than when he had had nothing? Had not the money only made him more tired, more weary than he had ever been before?

Was he not now more than ever conscious of his ninety-seven years? All because of the worry? … Well nearly all because of the money?

Patrick O'Hennessey never did reach ninety-eight. He died a few short weeks later; just seven days before his birthday. Some said of a broken heart. Others said of a broken … well there's no need to go into that here.

They buried him where he had always lived; in the steep valley that few other men seldom visited. And in the town that lay below the old women were quiet, for a part of them had died too. For a part of Patrick O'Hennessey had been in all of them …

THE END

20
SONGS

If music be the food of love ... well, I must have got indigestion! Four love songs to enchant any wooing couple ...

1. The Romanian Love Song

TRANSLATED BY A NOT VERY GOOD TRANSLATOR

Every day of my life
I have searched up and in
For a boy with such charismatically attractive
   physical properties.
Then when you erected yourself
Right into my life
I knew you were the one boy for me.

Oh boy,
I want to maintain you,
To feel your increases in temperature right next
   to me,

Oh boy,
You're such a delirious character,
I want to inject our love
With responsive involvement.

On that night we first met,
We walked in the arboretum,
Our special involvement was intentionally
   rampant,
Then when you invaded your love,
Exceptionally deep,
I knew that you were that hot cake for me.

Oh boy,
I want to reflect you,
You make my metabolic cycle go exceptionally
   high.
Oh boy,
You're so delightfully merry,
I want to expand you in several directions
At the same time.

Boy you're so insertive,
Boy you're so ejective,
Boy you're so exceptionally throbful,
Boy you're so keyboards,
Boy you're so reliable,
Boy you're compulsively large.

You were so shy, so proportional,

101

So particularly thrusting at me.
When you rolled your eyeballs directionally
I knew you were the one
To respond to my nibble
And engage in an act of
sexual
disenfranchisementisation.

2. The Anti-love Song

Girl, when I met you
I knew this must be love.
You offered me your hand, dear,
I gave you a big shove.
I said I adored you,
I squeezed you to my chest —
You started to go purple
And have cardiac arrest.

Feelings like these
Are hard to explain,
Please say you love me
Or I'll blow out your brain.

I took you to dinner —
Romantic interlude,
White wine and roses,
Soft lighting — fine food,
I softly embraced you,

Promised you my heart,
As our lips met, dear,
I had a big f-
    f-eelings like these
Are hard to restrain,
Please say you love me,
Or I'll push you under a train.

3. Greensleeves (Trad.)

This traditional love song has never sounded better than in this new updated version.

The girl I loved,
She meant all to me,
Her skin was pure,
Felt like ivory.
Her hair was gold,
And her nose it ran,
And she never went out
With a hanky,
Greensleeves
Was my name for her ...

4. The Grammatical Song
— an Irish Love Song

The girl that I marry —
I'd like her to be
The shape of a well-formed apostrophe;
Together we'd conjugate,
We'd have colons and syntax
We'd both punctuate.

The girl that I marry —
I have no doubt,
Will have curvy brackets, a large umlaut.
She'd have a silent pee,
Her eyes would have dots and a slash on her
    tee.

The girl that I marry —
Will be round and dark,
A nice little blob like a question mark.
A dipthong here and there,
And as for her full stops
She'd have a nice pair ...

21
SPERM DONORS

Where sexual partners should prove unavailable or unacceptable you might try the local sperm donor clinic as a cheap alternative to your normal love-making!

Donor 1: Is this your first time?

Donor 2: Mmmm.

Donor 1: Me too ... nervous?

Donor 2: A bit.

Donor 1: What made you ...?

Donor 2: Want to give sperm ...?

Donor 1: Mmmm.

Donor 2: Dunno really ... got a bit bored giving blood and just fancied a change I suppose. Couldn't give my liver, or my heart ... yet. They wouldn't take my rectum. Not unless I was a practising freemason. So there wasn't much else left to give ...

Funny thing that about being a donor,
the things they do and don't want you
to give.

Donor 1: Well, that's right ... I mean take ear
wax, I must have got bucketsful of the
stuff lined up at home ... find anyone
to take it? Not a chance ... even the
WAR ON WANT shop turned me down
and they usually take anything ... Or
belly button fluff ... how come you can
never donate your old belly button fluff
to no one?

Donor 2: Suppose it's not much use, that's why.

Donor 1: Well, they could stick it all together
and give it away to bald people to
cover the gaps.

Donor 2: Can't see it ... I mean, would you want
to go around with the contents of
another person's navel stuck to the top
of your bonce?

Donor 1: They'd probably wash it first ... take
out all the matted bits that smelt like
fish paste ... be quite attractive when
they'd finished.

Donor 2: A bit like one of them ethnic hearth
rugs.

Donor 1: S'right ... or take spots ...

Donor 2: No, I don't think they do.

Donor 1: Exactly, and why don't they? Why not
a National Spot Transfusion service

going round the country encouraging spotties to come forward and donate a few pustules for the unblemished, squeeze a few in when you're feeling poxy, draw them out again when your complexion clears up?

Donor 2: MacDonalds is always full of pretty scabby people.

Donor 1: It's not the same though is it ... it's not official ... it doesn't say 'National Scab Transfusion Service' on the door does it? It doesn't say 'please squeeze your buboils out into this' on one of the relish trays, does it? Or take verrucas, why can't you become a verruca donor?

Donor 2: Well, who'd want old verrucas, then?

Donor 1: I always did, at school ... I used to lie in bed at night for hours praying to God to give me a verruca ... so I wouldn't have to do swimming next day ... all I ever got was acne and a wart on the end of my nose, and that didn't stop me swimming, it just gave me somewhere to hang my towel when I got out of the water.

Donor 2: Funny isn't it, the things you can't give away, you can't give away pimples ...

Donor 1: Or boils ...

Donor 2: Or bogies ...

Donor 1: You can't go out and become a registered bogey donor.

Donor 2: Not unless you join the Young Conservatives.

Donor 1: You can't carry round a little card with 'snot donor' printed on it.

Donor 2: Or display a little car sticker with 'I Gave Gob Today'.

Donor 1: You can't parcel off your old toe clippings to the world's needy.

Donor 2: And have you tried offering anyone any old bum fluff recently? Take in a big bagful and they show you the door.

Donor 1: And a bucket.

Donor 2: Hang about ... looks like you're in ... have one for me while you're in there ...!!!

THE CELIBATE PAGES

Throughout this book helpful advice and assist-
ance has been offered to those with sexual problems or questions. We offer herewith a section
especially for celibate readers. If you have no
sexual interests or wish to avoid sex then turn to
these pages in the book and insert a book mark.
Whenever you feel a little bit randy you need
simply open at the book mark to find pages
which contain nothing of an erotic nature and
your sexual passions will be quelled at once.

The great speeches of Winston Churchill

The authenticated first draft of the compendium
of Churchill's great speeches.

GUARANTEE:
THIS PAGE CONTAINS
• NOTHING •
OF A SEXUAL NATURE

~~Never in the course of history~~
~~was so much owed by me~~
~~to my milkman~~

~~Never in the course of history~~
~~was so much owed by so many~~
~~to my milkman~~

~~Never in the course of history~~
~~was so much owed by so many~~
~~to ME!~~

~~Never in the course of history~~
~~was so much owed by so many~~
~~to me and my lucky rabbits foot~~

~~Never in the course of history was~~
~~so much owed by me to~~
~~Jane Russell~~
~~Jane Russell~~   ~~Jane Russell~~
~~Jane Russell~~ ~~Jane Russell~~
~~Jane Russell~~
~~Dear Jane~~

GUARANTEED NON-EROTIC

~~Dearest Jane~~

~~My~~ Dear Jane ~~Jane my Dearest~~

~~Dear Cuddles Jane~~

~~Dear Sneaky Pops~~

~~Dear Sexy~~ ~~Jane~~ Sizzling Jane

~~I'm a very important Prime Minister
of England and I wondered if we
could have a good time together~~

→ Never in the course of history
was so much owed by so many to
↘ SO FEW!

this one

~~Winston Churchill~~
Prime Minister
Aged 63¾

GUARANTEE:
THIS PAGE CONTAINS
• NOTHING •
OF A SEXUAL NATURE

The celibate unusual fact sheet

Avoid all erotic feelings with these thirty specially non-arousing facts.

GUARANTEE
THIS PAGE CONT
• NOTHING •
OF A SEXUAL NA

1. William Shakespeare didn't invent the biro.
2. No one was eaten alive by a badger last year.
3. Napoleon never passed a driving test.
4. You don't have to have a licence to own a table tennis bat.
5. Maggots won't sing if you soak them in chloride.
6. If you point a piece of copper due south and leave it overnight it will still be in the same position next day.
7. It takes an average of eleven players ninety minutes to play an ordinary game of football.
8. Superman's middle name wasn't Terry.
9. An earthworm doesn't transmit 4000 volts every time it sneezes.
10. Louis XVI never owned a flat in the Barbican.
11. Anagrams weren't invented as a by-product of nuclear warfare.
12. You can't get pregnant through eating too much toast.
13. If you rub a ham sandwich into your hair

you won't go bald.

(That's to say it won't make you go bald. It won't actually stop you going bald if you're heading that way — sorry, just thought we ought to get it straight — Ed.)

14. Edward Heath is not a twin sister of Helen Shapiro.

15. Winston Churchill could not play the electric organ and didn't have a cabaret act where he sawed a live chicken in half.

16. If you travel by London Transport every day then after ten years you'll have travelled by London Transport quite a bit.

17. The Spanish for 'wholewheat bread' isn't 'el ricot'.

18. If you spit ever so slightly into the bottom of a breathalyser just before you blow it up then you'll probably only make things worse for yourself.

19. Eva Peron was never involved in the planning of the Docklands Light Railway scheme.

20. In Finnish criminal law there is nothing to stop you going to sleep in your own kitchen.

21. If you laid everyone who took 'O'-levels last year down in a long line then it would probably take you quite a long time to collect up all the papers.

22. Arthur Mullard didn't win the men's singles

at Wimbledon in 1958.

23. If you write 'straight line' backwards it spells 'enil thgiarts'.

24. The Bible doesn't once mention 'Stockport County'.

25. Brian Clough has had several colds during his lifetime.

26. If you walked from the end of one wing of a Jumbo jet to the end of the other then you'd probably be arrested.

27. Fifty-six times twenty is always one thousand one hundred and twenty.

28. Pigeons can't fly upside down.

29. The Edgware Road literally means 'the road going to Edgware'.

30. Michelangelo's brother was not a bicycle repair shop owner.

GUARANTEED NON-EROTIC

Take your mind off carnal yearnings with:

THE IRISH GOAL-OF-THE-MONTH CONTEST

GOAL A Scored by MacMurphy of Ballyshannon Athletic against Ballyshannon Athletic in the match between Ballyshannon Athletic and Patrick Thistle.

GOAL C Scored by MacMurphy for Bally-shannon Athletic in the match between Shamrock Rovers and Hearts of Dungannon.

GOAL F A left-footed header by MacMurphy for Ballyshannon Athletic in the match that never took place between Ballyshannon Athletic and the local post-mistress.

GOAL B Scored by MacMurphy for Bally-shannon Rovers in the nil-all draw against Ballyshannon Rovers.

GOAL B Scored by MacMurphy for Bally-shannon Athletic in next week's match between Ballyshannon Rovers and Ballyshannon Athletic and Ballyshannon Rovers.

TO ENTER: PUT YOUR NAME, AGE AND ADDRESS ON THE INSIDE OF AN OLD ENVELOPE, PUT *IRISH GOAL OF THE MONTH, IRISH TV, GLASGOW* ON THE ENVELOPE, PUT A STAMP INSIDE THE ENVELOPE. SEAL IT UP, AND FORGET TO SEND IT ANYWHERE.

GUARANTEE:
THIS PAGE CONTAINS
• NOTHING •
OF A SEXUAL NATURE

CLASSIFIED ADVERTISEMENTS

A MAN STANDS BY HIS DOG AS IT CHEWS AWAY ON A BOWL OF DOGGO ... THE NEW MEATY DOG FOOD

V.O.: Reg Humphries has been breeding with championship poodles now for over twenty years.

REG SMILES CONTENTEDLY AND PATS THE DOG ON ITS HEAD

V.O.: ... isn't it about time he packed it in before someone calls the police???

When you want to feel like this
Then you need

NAVVIE!

Navvie is more than just a deodorant, more than just an anti-perspirant ... Navvie is real globules of

NAVVIE SWEAT scraped dew-fresh from the armpit of a passing Irish building worker, collected together in an old dirty milk bottle and mixed with the cheesy bits from between a navvie's toes.

NAVVIE!

Smells like real navvie's sweat
Just splash it on all over
Without taking your jacket off

Now in three great varieties
Irish/Algerian/Greek Cypriot

Navvie! ... for real men

JUST LOOK FOR THE BOGEY FLOATING AROUND INSIDE THE BOTTLE!!!

Blow-up mothers-in-law

Made from finest simulated pink quilted nylon. Pop into the bed. Guaranteed against ALL sharp objects. Stain-proof. One for £4.90, three for £12.00 CUPID SEX AIDES, The Nolan Sister Industrial Estate, Dun Laoghaire.

Naughty Robin leaking hotty

Guaranteed to take the love out of love making! THREE exciting colours: OFF YELLOW, OFF PURPLY-GREEN, VERY OFF WHITE! Made from perished, sensitized latex rubber with CARD-BOARD cap. The NAUGHTY ROBIN leaks the moment you move. Improve your abstinence by weeks! A real turn-off! Box 198.

Bondage can be fun
— but so can accountancy

At ACCOUNTANCY LINK-UP we have over 2,000 chartered accountancy personnel to choose from; outings, travel, marriage, own ledger. Meet more friends! Get more letters! Audit more accounts! The IDEAL way to keep your mind off SEX. Write ACCOUNTANCY LINK-UP, Ballymakellyskeelennis for full details — marking your envelope 'Norma Smeere Massage Parlour & High Quality Love Nest'.

Only a few now left!
— navy blue serge knickers

Also a limited stock of matching green and yellow bobble hats. A must for all non-liberated women.
Sizes: LARGE, V. LARGE, OUTSIZE.
No callers please. Ring three times (and ask for Sister O'Keefe).

Books! Books! Books! — New!!!

THE SENSUAL PROPERTY DEVELOPER, LADY CHATTERLEY'S LIVER (with sixty-four full page anatomical line diagrams), VISUAL DICTIONARY OF EROTIC AEROMODELLING ... and many many more ... 'RODRIGUES', c/o The Monastery of St Benedickt and St Mark.

Topless buses

Ideal for the unromantic holidays. Buy a day-long ROVER TICKET. Unlimited mileage, unlimited company, unlimited opportunities to avoid sexual advances ...!

Nausea drops

Slip into her Hot Bovril before going to put the cat out. Works by actually TRAINING THE MIND to feel really horrible. 'Hubby slept in the kiddies' room for over a week afterwards' — Mrs O'L., Dublin ... 'We don't even shave together any more' — Mrs O'A.-P, Cork ... 'I can honestly say I've never felt so appalling ... thanks to you' — Mrs O'K., Killkeel*.
NAUSEA DROPS are approved by the BMQ. Scientifically proven under lavatory conditions.

NAUSEA DROPS!!!
* *Authentic statements.*

Saucy sausage dinner

Replica meal of egg, whelk, and sausage made from lubricated soft vinyl. Powerful vibrating action (batteries not included) makes the food actually SLIDE ABOUT THE PLATE! Place on bedside table! Knock off bedside table onto bed itself ... the instant turn-off! Ideal for getting rid of naughty party-goers. SWITCH ON DURING MATCH OF THE DAY AND WATCH YOUR SUITOR'S ADVANCES STOP. Also available in Kosher, Vegetarian and Low Calorie. Box No. 198761423572184.

Ask for a new sensation in sauna or massage

at the 'KNUCKLES' MALONE SPORTSMAN'S GYM ... for the DEAD BUTCH only!

RUBBERWEAR

Exclusive import from Bulgaria. RUBBER UNDER-SHEETS — We have just managed to obtain a few specially made heavy-duty SMESNOVITCH UNDERSHEETS. As seen in the film CONFESSIONS OF A GERIATRIC DOMICILIARY. Moves with you! Crimples during sex! Pokes in at least six annoying places (not Tipperary). Rasps if you move against it. Hours of irritation. Recommended for honey-moons, amorous au pairs, door-to-door salesmen. Buy now while stocks last!!!

Camphor cream

Rub it on all over before making tea. Rub it on all over before taking your clothes off. Rub it on again all over after taking your clothes off. Rub into bed-clothes. Used liberally CAMPHOR CREAM completely takes the mind off anything sexy. Get a good night's sleep. As seen on radio! 'NON COITUS', Wogan Avenue, Drogheda.

The Sir Lancelot

The Sir Lancelot chastity belt fits neatly round the whole of the man's body to remove even the slightest chance of contact. Made from finest Swedish pitch pine. Takes over THREE HOURS to assemble! Keeps you both occupied till the small hours. You will both be so dead-beat there's ABSOLUTELY NO CHANCE of even HEAVY PETTING. The De Luxe Sir Lancelot keeps you up till morning (240 watt power attachment extra). You won't even have to sleep together! No fun ... or your money refunded in full ...!

Crutchless deerstalker

As worn by countless TV celebrities (Male/Female/Other). Ask for Thompson's Crutchless Deerstalker by name! Absolutely no sign of a crutch in this scantiest of hats! Shock and Amaze your friends. Don't be misled by imitations. With exciting BUILT-IN ear muffles. Wear it if you dare!!!

EASY TO USE INDEX

There, see — that was easy to use, wasn't it?
Nothing there — nothing to look up — easiest index
I've ever seen!!!

IF AFTER ALL ELSE YOU STILL FAIL TO SCORE THEN FORGET THE WHOLE THING AND CON-CENTRATE ON BINGO INSTEAD

IRISH BINGO CARD

Cut out and keep for your next Bingo session:

1	2	3	4	5	6	7	8	9	10	11	12	13	14	15
16	17	18	19	20	21	22	23	24	25	26	27	28	29	30
31	32	33	34	35	36	37	38	39	40	41	42	43	44	45
46	47	48	49	50	51	52	53	54	55	56	57	58	59	60
61	62	63	64	65	66	67	68	69	70	71	72	73	74	75
76	77	78	79	80	81	82	83	84	85	86	87	88	89	90
91	92	93	94	95	96	97	98	99	X	X	X	X	X	X

THE IRISH BINGO CARD

* Contains every number called

* No chance of winning but at least you're kept busy trying.

A
BACKWARD

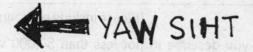 THIS WAY

DID YOU FIND THIS BOOK USEFUL?

Please remove this page from the book and return to the address below having completed the answers below.

Did you find this book useful? _____
(Please include diagram)

What portion of the book did you find most useful?

_____

_____
(Please include photographs)

Can you describe in not less than 50,000 words your experiences with your partner after reading this book?

_____
(Use second sheet if necessary)

Has it cleared up yet? _____
(Please supply evidence)

Would you be willing to pose topless for a new monthly magazine on Church Architecture? _____
(Sorry, no choirmasters need apply)

Return to:

The All Irish Sex Association
Bonkers House, Been Avenue,
Dublin, Scotland.